How to Loosen Up Your Painting

Malcolm Dewey

How to Loosen Up Your Painting

Malcolm Dewey

Published by Malcolm Dewey, 2016.

Copyright

Table of Contents

How to Loosen Up Your Painting 1

Your Brushes 21

Use More Paint 27

Painting in acrylics 44

A Painting in Oils 52

Outdoor Figure Study 61

To Kerrin and the boys My daily motivation

Introduction

There are myriad forms of creative endeavor, each with its own unique allure. Take painting, for instance. It encompasses a vast array of styles and genres, each offering a gateway to a world of endless exploration. Yet, even after a lifetime of immersion, there remains an inexhaustible well of knowledge to be tapped. This is the beauty of creativity-a profound insight into the boundless potential of our minds, a portal to the universe of possibilities.

Creativity is a powerful state of being—perhaps limitless if you consider the forces that run through our universe. What does that have to do with artists like you and me? Well, we are part of the universe. We are creative by nature, and this is where humans show their unique and special place in the universe. We create not only out of necessity but also for the pleasure of the process.

It should be easy, then. Sadly not. But we can fix that.

Loose painting is relatively new. Born out of the Industrial Revolution in the mid-1800s, the result was a changed society. The rise of a leisured middle-class with money to spare for painting. Plus, the technology that produced ready-mixed paint in tubes. Then, the desire to break away from the rigid past and embrace a new form of painting. Painting from real life. The banalities of everyday activities were now fit subjects for art.

New artists shook up the establishment. First came Corot, then Millet, Manet, and the leader of impressionism, Claude Monet. The revolution had begun. Painting loose and expressively was now desirable.

Why Loosen Up?

Many artists feel nervous about their painting ability. If you are a beginner, this may seem reasonable, but why so? This confidence issue can last for years—needlessly!

Consequently, you feel that your painting is tight—maybe even boring. At least to you, there is no spark to your painting, and this frustrates you. Maybe you have reached your talent limit. After all, look at those other paintings that other artists produce—full of life, color, and joy.

Stop!

Before you pack away your paints, you need to face the truth. You can change your style and free up your painting. But first:

To paint loose, you need the following:

1. Self-confidence
2. Working knowledge of painting fundamentals
3. A few techniques and tools
4. Practice

That is all. You have the talent, but you need to channel that talent along the correct path. Focus on what matters. Then see the change in your art happen very quickly.

The Mind Change

I am not going directly into techniques and equipment. To do so would be wasting your time. You see, painting loose is a skill that needs to be learned. But you will only learn when you are in the correct mind state. Or should I say when your mind is not playing tricks on you by telling you to paint within the lines? Another example of the mind undermining you is to tell you that loose painting is sloppy. It is actually quite a challenge, as Impressionist artists discovered. There are many other blocks in mindset that I cover in greater detail in my "creativity book" series.

The ideal state of mind is called Flow. When you are in a state of flow, you are entirely absorbed in the moment's joy. When Usain Bolt is sprinting for that gold medal, he is not thinking about paying the bills or sending a text message. When an artist is in the flow of creating it feels like the picture is painting itself!

You cannot get into the flow state when you are anxious about how the painting will turn out.

Or worrying about wasting paint.

Or what your significant other will say.

Or what to wear to work tomorrow.

You need to show up with an uncluttered mind and start. So, step one is to **be aware** of what your mind is doing. See those negative thoughts? Throw them out. They do not define you. The thoughts are trying to protect you from imaginary fears. Dismiss imaginary things because they do not exist unless you believe them to be real. Change your thoughts – change your reality.

If it helps, try to write down all the obstacles to your painting desires. Look at those reasons and decide how likely they are to happen. How flimsy they are. Would you listen to these objections if, for example, your child's health was a stake? Or getting that job? Or paying the utility bill? Of course not. You would get these things done. So, too, is your creative life at risk due to imaginary fears.

Your Resolution: Once you have accepted that you are worthy and can change your painting outcomes, you must resolve to change. Tell yourself that you will relax and do what is necessary to learn and practice your new style. Persistence and determination are key.

Set small goals that are achievable. For example, you will:

● Try one painting a month in the new loose approach. At least one painting. No exceptions.

● Look up new lessons, classes, or courses on the loose painterly style; for example, my course How to Loosen Up Your Painting will be helpful (find links in the About Author section);

● Seek out mentors or other artists experienced enough to inspire you;

Then, practice what you learn. Accept your mistakes as necessary stepping stones on the journey.

Now, you will be able to make real progress.

The Language of Painting

A loose painting style does not mean throwing the rules out of the window; far from it. Even abstract painters know the rules of painting. Or, as I prefer to call it – the language of painting.

What is the Language of Painting?

Your spoken language enables you to speak, sing, write different things, and generally communicate in many ways. Similarly, the language of painting allows you to paint in many different styles and genres. Also, you can depict any subject that you want.

The building blocks of spoken language include the alphabet, grammar, and many styles of language construction. In painting, these building blocks cover topics like values, color, composition, brushwork, and much more.

Once you grasp the language of painting, you can create any kind of painting you can imagine.

Unfortunately, these fundamentals are seldom taught at school or even at the tertiary level. Everyone is being taught conceptual thinking without any foundation to build on. No wonder these artists graduate without knowing how to paint a landscape. For example, a change is coming with the growth of plein air painting. These fundamentals are now in demand.

What does the language of painting have to do with painting loose?

For a painting to have an impact and communicate something to the viewer, you still need to use these basics to make the painting work. Loose painting relies upon these basics because you are not painting fine details. You are painting large shapes arranged in a way that the viewer's eye can interpret as something in the real world.

This is the beauty of the loose style. You are not presenting a photo-realistic painting. You are presenting a painting made up of abstract shapes arranged so the viewer's eye and brain can interpret them. This increases the pleasure for the viewer since there is some mystery that needs interpretation. Also, it is fascinating to see how different artists interpret the same scene differently using loose styles. No painting is ever the same.

Learn the Basics

Needless to say, you will need to learn the basics of value, color, composition, line, and edges, among others. Practice these and develop your brushwork signature over time.

My course, *Learn to Paint With Impact*, will help you learn these fundamentals through practical exercises. Find out more in the About Author section below.

Whatever way you choose to learn, make sure it is based on consistent practice.

Simplification of the Subject

The most important skill to learn is how to simplify a subject. You can call this **learning to see like an artist.**

For example, the average landscape consists of so many varying shapes, colors, and values that the beginner is left with one conclusion. Paint everything and hope for the best. Sadly this almost never works out. The result is often a meaningless arrangement of things that communicates nothing. When everything is given equal treatment in a painting you are left with a dull result. There can be no democracy in a painting. Something must dominate the rest, while other things must be ruthlessly excluded.

Tips to Simplify?

1. **Squint a little**. By half-closing your eyes, you can see details disappear into light and dark shapes. The values of light and dark are easier to consider.
2. Use **notan** drawings to record this process.
3. Follow up with **thumbnail sketches** to set down the composition.

Practice making starts on a small panel or canvas. Even your drawing pad can be used with acrylics or gouache.

I have a few more thoughts on the idea of learning to see like an artist. When I first studied the Impressionists in my high school art class, I was fascinated by the colors, brushwork, and the ability these artists had to change an everyday scene into something beautiful. The Old Masters, for the most part, painted allegorical scenes, mythology, and Biblical stories. On the other hand, the Impressionists observed everyday life in a new way. I understood that they were not simply looking for new ways with the brush and colors. They were **seeing** the beauty in those scenes. In a way, these artists were guiding us to see the world differently, too.

Take note: there is beauty all around. We have to observe, interpret, and create.

What are Values?

Although this book is not intended to explain the fundamentals of painting in great detail, I want to introduce you to the big topics. Values are so important that I want you to learn more about them. At times referred to as Tone, values mean the **degree of light and dark in shapes and color.**

Imagine a black-and-white photograph. The gradations on the grey scale are measured as values. This example also illustrates that values are the foundation of a painting. Remove the color, and you still have a picture.

Values are conveniently divided into ten degrees of light and dark. The Munsell value scale isolates the ten gradations.

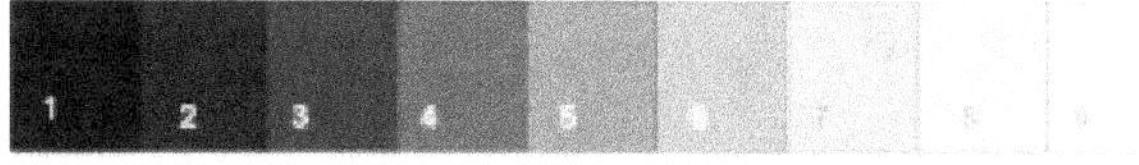

Image 1 The Munsell Value Scale

If you hold up the value scale and compare it to a shape in your reference scene, you should be able to discern the degree of light or dark in the shape. Your painted shape should correspond. Of course, the trick is to see value in colors. After all, we see it in color, not black and white. However, if you can accurately distinguish light and dark shapes, you will keep those relationships intact when you mix colors.

Remember that strong light and dark patterns make a strong, interesting painting. **Look for values first.**

Color

Yes, color delights every artist. Color has so much potential in the hands of an artist like you. But does it also scare you? In the beginning, the thought of mixing colors is daunting. So beginners opt to buy tube colors in every hue. This is an expensive mistake and will hold you back.

Rather, purchase the primary colors and white. Cadmium red, Cadmium yellow, ultramarine blue, and titanium white form the backbone of most artist's colors. With these colors, you will learn the essentials of color mixing and seeing values in color.

Of course, you can add convenience colors like burnt sienna and yellow ochre. But please study color mixing with the primary colors. It will boost your confidence if you can mix your burnt sienna and yellow ochre. You will be amazed at the variety of warm and cool tones you can get by mixing your earth colors. When you have these skills you can opt to use tubes of burnt sienna and yellow ochre to save time. The nice thing is that you can easily vary their value and color temperature with the knowledge gained from color mixing.

Basic Color Terms to Remember:

- **Hue** - the name of the color e.g., Cadmium red light

- **Saturation** - The degree of concentration or intensity of pigment. The paint in the tube is at its highest saturation.

- **Value** - the degree of light and dark as per the Munsell value scale (Tone means much the same, but use value instead)

- **Temperature** - the relative warmth or coolness of the color compared to another color.

- **The key is the degree of brightness of the colors. For example, neon orange is high-key compared to olive green, which is low-key. A low-key painting will be dark, and a high-key painting will be** lighter overall.

- **Tint** – to mix white into a color and lighten it

- **Shade** – to darken a color

Color Wheel:

Obtain a color wheel and learn the basics of complementary, analogous, and split complementary colors.

These elements of the color wheel are not all easy to grasp right away. That is not a problem. As you grow in knowledge and experience, you will discover new ways to use the color wheel practically. Please do not bore yourself with color theory! Far more important to get brush time!

If you are beginning, then **focus on the following:**

1. Know the primary colors.
2. Know the complementary colors.
3. Know secondary colors
4. Understand that color has value.
5. Color has a temperature when compared to another color.

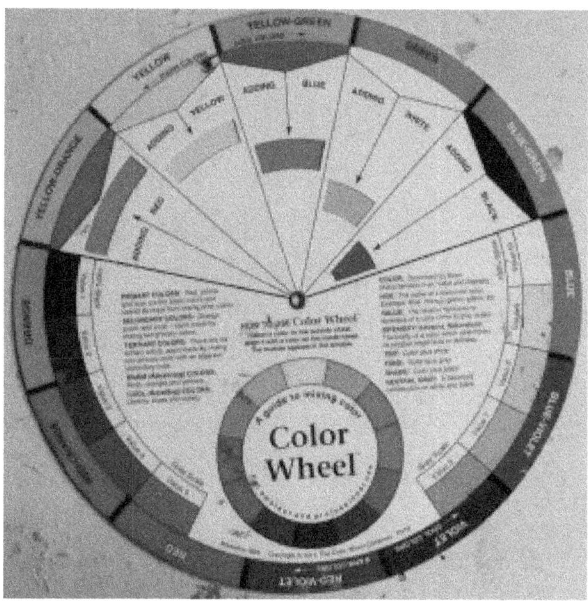

Suggested color wheel

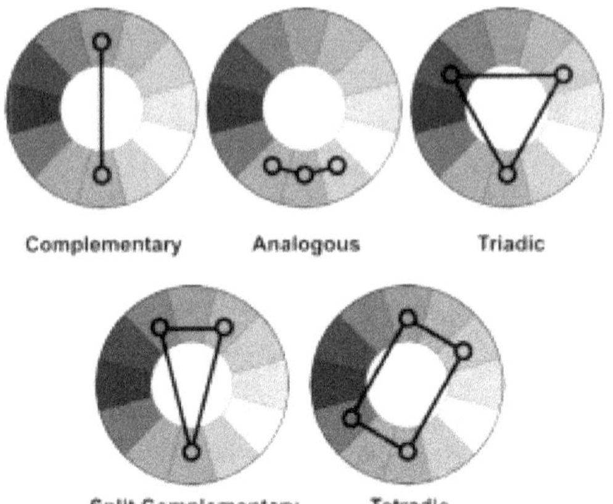

Basic Color Combinations

Color Temperature

Yes, color has a temperature. It is a vital part of understanding color. Sure, you know that yellow is warm and blue is cool. Despite this knowledge, when artists start painting from nature, they easily miss the significance of color temperature.

Why is this?

You do not see many primary colors when you look at Mother Nature. Most of nature's colors are neutrals. We call these colors "grays" not because they are a mix between black and white but because they are mixes of primary, secondary, or tertiary colors. You will hear yourself saying, "That tree has a cool bluish/violet shadow color." Then, you need to try and mix that color.

Often, artists see a shadow, for example, and use a dark brown hue to depict the shadow. It looks odd, though, because the brown, while darker than the sunlit brown, is still warm. In reality, the shadow is comprised of cool reflected light if it is put against another color. Cool light leans to the shadow colors like cool blues and violets. These colors will read correctly as shadows to the viewer. The Impressionists discovered this feature of color with scientific discoveries of the day.

Variation in color temperature helps your loose painting style suggest information to the viewer. It is part of the communication between the painting and the viewer. That "language" thing again!

Remember that color temperature is relative. One color may be objectively warm, but put it against another color and it may seem cool.

Look at relationships between one color note and the next and ask yourself if it is warmer or cooler. Adjust your color mix accordingly. Remember to adjust the color temperature for aerial perspective. Color becomes cooler, and values become lighter over distance.

How do you warm color? By adding a warm color to the mix. How do you cool a color? Yes, by adding a cool color to the mix. It can be that simple. By making color charts you can see the gradations of color from warm to cool. This is something to practice, although it takes commitment and patience. The result will be a chart that you can refer to as a reminder of what, for example, a desaturated blue looks like.

White Paint:

Always be careful when adding titanium white to your mix. Too much white is difficult to remove from a mix. Always add white little by little to adjust the value. The problem is that titanium white is a cold, chalky color. It will make your colors cold and weak very easily. Dark shadows, for example, should not have any white added; keep them dark and slightly transparent. When mixing lights, on the other hand, decide how warm they need to be. Warm lights will have white and yellow, for example. Not just white. Cool lights will have, for example, white and blue or white and violet in the mix. Not just white. So you see that white is a powerful desaturating color that makes color cooler and lightens values.

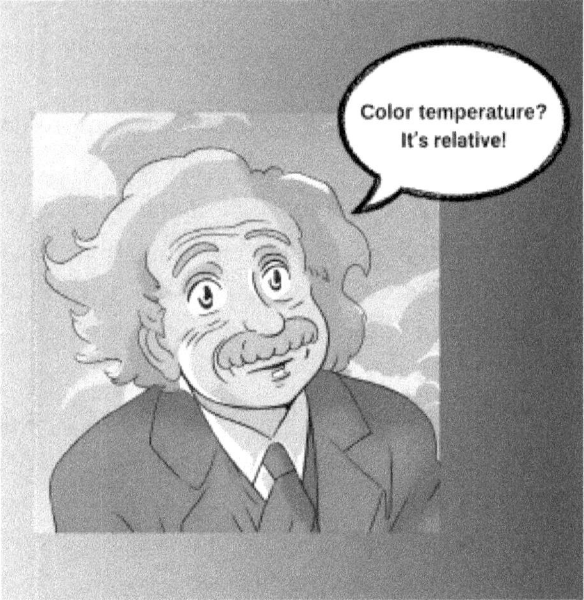

Who can argue with Einstein!

Edges and Brushwork

Edges:

The concept of edges is one of the keys to loose painting. If all edges are equally defined, then the shapes in the painting will be more like illustrations. This is clear, for instance, in a comic where all images have a distinct dark outline. Fine art, however, does not use this method. Edges help to suggest something to the viewer.

For example, a tree is a three-dimensional object. To convey this illusion to the viewer, the artist may have to soften the edges on one side of the tree's shape.

Another example is something inherently soft, like hair. The edges around a portrait's head will be softened to suggest the hair accurately.

Hard edges convey certain facts, too. The edge of a roof may be crisp and stark, but a hard edge can also emphasize a focal point. **Remember** that your eye will see hard edges first before noticing softer edges. Use this fact to catch the eye and direct the viewer to the focal point.

Brushwork:

Variation of brushwork is necessary to convey hard or soft edges. The manner of holding the brush and the pressure of brush strokes are skills to practice. Soften hard lines by brushing over the edge of a shape, thereby blending the hard line.

Vary the pressure you apply to a brushstroke to vary the volume of paint on that edge.

Edges can also be softened or emphasized with **value** contrast or **color contrast.** A dark shape against a light shape will naturally result in a hard edge, which is great for dramatic counterchange.

Also, a color may contrast starkly with another color, although being of similar value. For example, red against green. In this case, the complementary color contrast attracts the eye.

An advanced tip to soften an edge is to use a transition color. For example, blue against white. Mix a third color using blue and white to create a lighter blue. Paint that lighter blue between the dark blue and white. The transition is now less stark. This is a basic explanation. You can see the potential to fettle those edges and colors using your brush and palette to good effect. Experiment. Make notes of your results.

Be aware of edges as your painting develops. Look at your brushstrokes and ask yourself, is there an edge that needs adjusting?

Stand back often to assess the painting as a whole. Look for edges or colors that are distracting. Adjust or remove offending elements.

Relationships

By now, you may have noticed that almost everything in a painting is based on relationships to other things. The values of shapes compared to other shapes, colors compared to other colors, and so on determine the painting. Look for relationships between shapes, and you will see where any corrections need to be made.

Ultimately, remember the words of the great impressionist Camille Pissaro, who said that artists must let nature be their guide. Look at the scene and be guided by what your eyes tell you. Paint what you see.

When mixing paint, ask the following questions: Lighter or darker, warmer or cooler?

"Don't be afraid of putting on color... Paint generously and unhesitatingly, for it is best not to lose the first impression."

Camille Pissarro

undefined

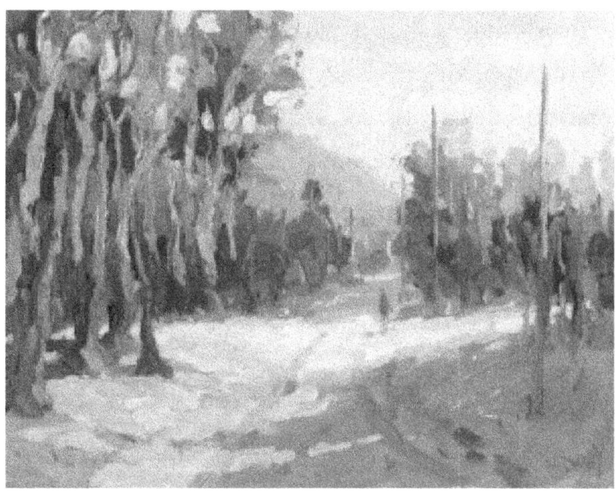

Warm and cool colors. Light and dark values. These combinations bring a painting to life.

Shapes

Finally, on the subject of the basics, I want to talk about shapes.

Loose painting means painting shapes, not details. Light and dark shapes make up the painting. Nothing else.

You may need to combine many light or dark shapes into a collection of light or dark shapes. This is called a "mass shape" of light or dark. We do this to avoid painting each dark or light leaf, for example. Instead, one mass shape suggests many leaves. Trust our mind to make sense of everything—our minds like simplicity.

Some shapes dominate, others are subordinate, and others are omitted entirely. This is the process of simplifying shapes. I spend a lot of time on this topic in my Learn to Paint with Impact course and for a good reason.

It is difficult to learn how to simplify a scene into essential shapes. We tend to put everything in and give everything equal importance. Perhaps this comes from using photographs so much instead of observation and memory.

As mentioned before, practice the **skill of squinting** to see basic shapes better. Leave out twigs and leaves. Paint the light and dark shapes.

This is a skill that will make you an artist before anything else.

Remember also that the brush makes shapes with each stroke. Use the brush to carve out shapes, either positive or negative, such as gaps between branches. Move the brush in the direction of the object's shape. This will leave a shape that echoes the actual shape of the object. For example, rounded brush strokes or swirling ones suggest moving water.

Can you identify the shapes of brushstrokes in the next painting?

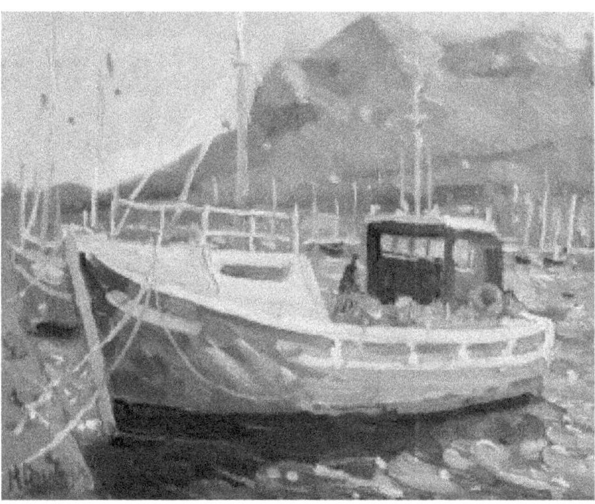

In the above example, I have treated colors, values, and edges.
Notice the following:

1. What attracts your eye first?
2. The light and dark counterchange? Why?
3. Warm and cool colors
4. Use of complementary color
5. Lack of detail in shapes, such as the sailors
6. Treatment of edges
7. Brushmarks - are they large or small and defined?
8. Color notes - such as shapes of color next to other shapes of color. How do these color shapes relate to each other?

Now, you can see how to use these elements to create a beautiful, loose painting. Loose does not mean sloppy.

A lot of knowledge has been put into this painting.

Now let us move on to tips for loose painting

Your Brushes

The brush does make a huge difference. Please keep the following in mind when you select a brush.

1. **Quality does make a difference**: Not to be a snob or anything, but better brushes do a better job. That being said, it is often difficult to find a good brush in the first place, especially if you are in a small center that does not cater to professional artists. You may have to order brushes. Is it worth the trouble and expense? You will need to decide depending on your stage in the learning curve. I only purchased professional brushes after a few years of effort to improve my basic skills. The difference in feel and workability of the brush was striking. My first professional brushes were from the Paris Classic range by Raphael, a manufacturer in France, and I still use their brushes today.

2. **Type of Brush?** There are two kinds of brush that the oil painter will consider. Bristle brushes or fine "sable" brushes. Have both on hand. You do not need genuine sable brushes, of course. A fine synthetic version may be sufficient. I am more interested in the effect that bristles, or fine hair has on the surface of the brushstroke. Bristle will leave more texture and abstraction to your shapes. Fine hair allows for softer blending but can also lay on buttery paint strokes.

3. **Size of Brush:** Bigger brush means bigger shapes and less detail. This should tell you why a large brush is desirable for loose painting. Why paint an object with thirty brushstrokes when three will do? Often, a painting is rescued when you discard the small brush and go over a fussy area with the large brush. You will see the abstract harmony emphasized and the fussy details disappear. Do I use small brushes? Yes, I have a Sable rigger brush for painting thin lines, like those for power lines, rigging on yachts, occasional grass shapes, small figures in a landscape, and signing my name on the painting.

1. **What Sizes?** This depends on the size of the painting. Generally, for a typical painting of 10 x 12", you would use size 6 and 8 brushes. If you

typically use a particular small-size brush, you can just go up two sizes and see if that helps.

2. **Use the Brush Handle:** Yes, of course, you know that, but I mean the full extent of the handle. Oil brushes have long handles so you can hold them while standing far back and still paint. This gives you a nice view of the entire painting. It also makes it difficult to finesse little shapes. You will be forced to put down large shapes by the very nature of the physical demands placed on you. If you persist despite the panic attacks, you will be pleasantly surprised by the end result.

3. **Shape of Brush:** Oil painting brushes come in three typical shapes: flat, filbert, and round. Fine liner brushes like riggers are used sparingly for a few details at the end. As far as the main shapes are concerned, I prefer flats and filberts. Plus, make sure you get the long-haired versions. Of the two, I prefer long flats for landscapes. Filberts are usually only long-haired and are great for portraits. These brushes are surprisingly versatile and can produce fine gestures if handled well.

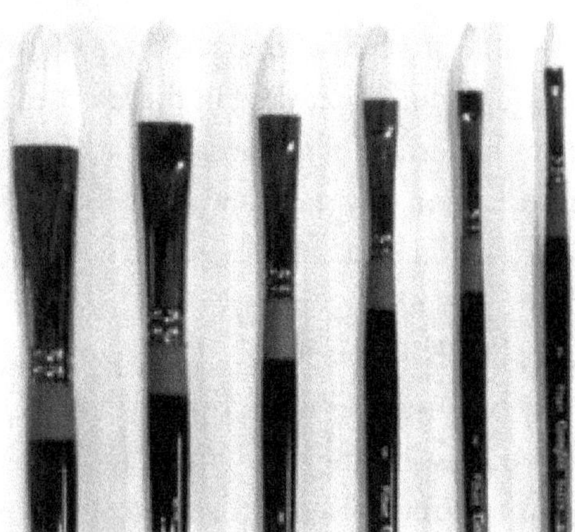

Filbert

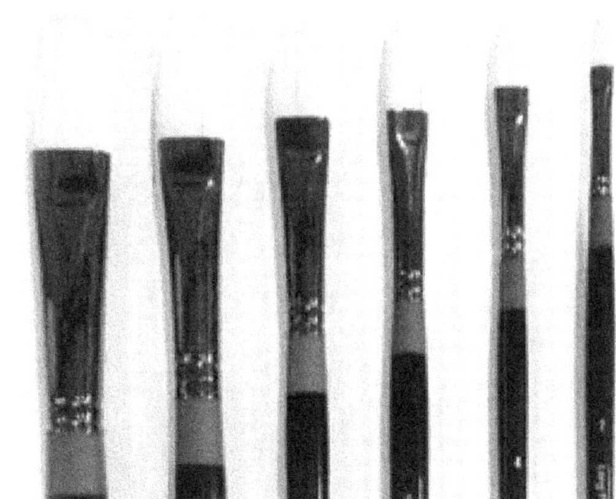

Long flat bristle

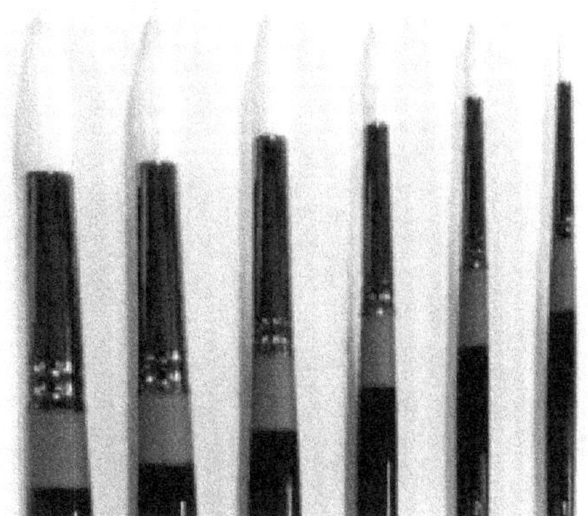

Round bristle brush

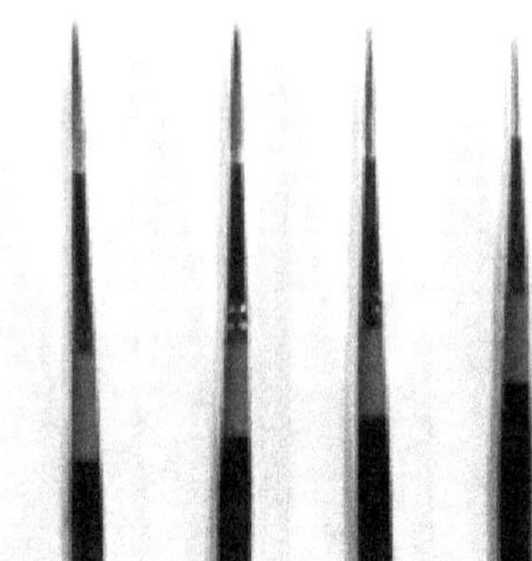

Sable rigger brushes

Stand and Paint

Standing will give you better loose painting results as tempting as it is to sit and paint. **If standing is impossible, si**t across a table (taboret) so that you need to stretch a bit to reach the canvas. Have your palette on the table before you to encourage the correct pose.

Standing encourages faster painting. It is not a race, but it keeps you energetic, and you tend to move along in your painting without laboring over details. Plus, it is easier to step back to view the overall abstract nature of your painting—how it all hangs together. Add music to the mix to get your groove thing going!

As discussed in the section on brushes, utilizing the length of the paintbrush handle can be a game-changer. This technique, combined with your outstretched arm, can create larger and more expressive shapes, giving you a new level of creative freedom and confidence.

Recognizing the signs of fatigue, such as a desire to sit, can be a cue for a well-deserved break. Painting is not just physically demanding but also mentally taxing, so it's crucial to prioritize self-care and take regular breaks.

Paint by the Pound

Use More Paint

One of the beautiful characteristics of oil paint is its shiny buttery quality. It simply begs to be layered onto your canvas with bravura brush strokes. Of course, you can use acrylics much the same.

Even watercolor benefits from layers, but the texture is entirely different.

There is no reward for being stingy with your paint. However, there are many benefits to generous paint application. They include:

- It provides texture to the surface. This creates interest and engagement when viewing the painting up close.

- It adds to the perception of skill. Collectors like to think that you are skilled and confident with your painting. This perception does enhance the aura of the painting.

- It can emphasize the elements of the painting. Rough surfaces, highlights against shadow, a sense of depth, and more can be accentuated.

- Colors are more complex. Color notes are also deeper, and more visual mixing occurs as color notes relate to each other. Think of the impressionist dabs of color notes next to each other.

- Paint can be moved and molded. The brush or painting knife can handle thick paint on the canvas. Objects like credit cards are sometimes used to push thick paint around, creating various effects. The experience of the "happy accident" happens more often this way.

Thick paint is not just for landscape or abstract painting. Portraits can also be created in dramatic yet sensitive ways with thick paint.

It is more challenging to paint an extensive work using thick paint since the sheer quantity of paint may alarm you. If so, I suggest painting in a smaller format, such as 10 x 12 or slightly more prominent.

This lets you complete the painting in generous layers without going through many tubes. The painting will look rich and glorious, and you will be proud of the result.

I'd like you to please consider this demo, where I discuss the use of thick paint.[1]

Using thick paint on small paintings also saves you money. Why is that? My experience has shown me that painting thin leads to paintings that are less vibrant, less interesting, and lacking that Impressionist joie de vivre that I am after. As a result, the paint expended has yet to create a wonderful painting. Instead, I feel cheated, and that is a waste of paint. When I apply paint in generous volume, the colors are brighter, there is texture and the experience of the painting as a whole is much more enjoyable. A rewarding experience for the viewer. This is paint well used.

If you have paint left over on your palette and your painting is complete, cover your palette overnight. Then, the next morning, have another look at the painting and use the rest of the paint by adding nice impasto swathes in the foreground, for example. The point is to use all the paint on your palette.

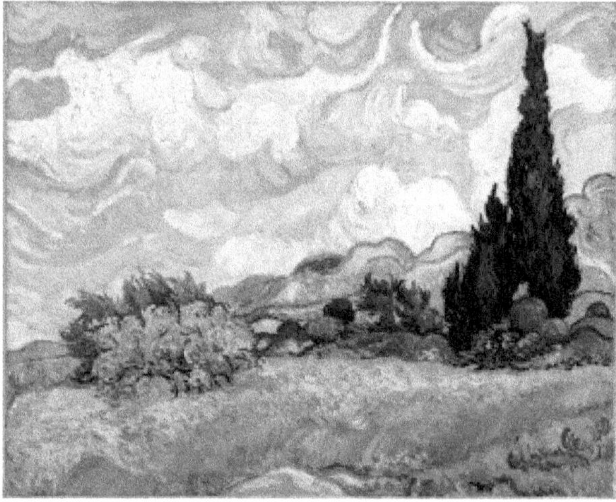

Van Gogh's Cypresses and Wheatfileds are a good example of generous use of paint volume and brushwork technique.

How to do this: Use your long flat bristle brush like a shovel. Scoop up a dollop of paint. Drag it over the canvas or dab it, much like you can imagine

---

1.   http://www.malcolmdeweyfineart.com/blog/artists-secrets-for-using-using-thick-paint-better

Van Gogh doing in the above example. Do not brush over that initial stroke, thereby ruining the texture.

No matter how tempted you are to blend the paint into flatness - resist this bad habit! Practice. You will get over old habits of blending your paint into smooth, dull painting surfaces.

Ignore the Details

As mentioned before, when isolating the values of a painting, use the squinting technique to look at a scene and eliminate all the details. Remember that a photo does not discriminate. It records everything, but this does not mean that you must paint everything in the photo.

Painting outdoors reduces this tendency due to the pressure of time and the immediacy of the subject. In the studio, you can fuss over details all too easily. Stop this habit and rather paint those large shapes of light and dark colors. I would consider the painting finished at this point. Even though you could continue refining and adding shapes. This overworking would defeat the object of getting a loose painting.

Determining your objective is important. As you can see from Claude Monet's painting, Impression Sunrise, he avoided much detail. A beginner would be tempted to include the many details in the busy scene, but the artist knew his objective and stuck to it. The result is perhaps one of the most famous works of the Impressionist era.

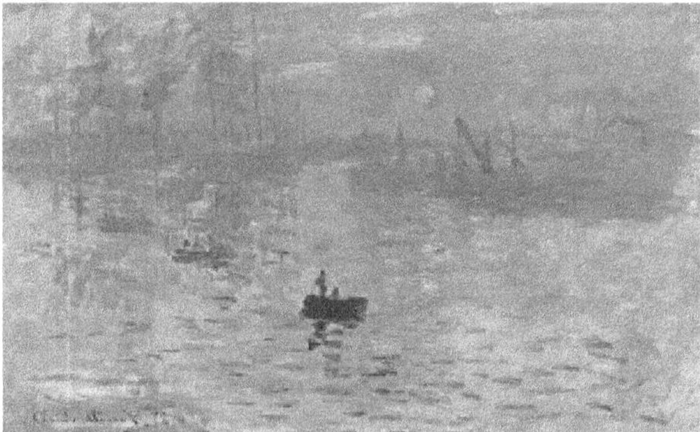

Claude Monet's Impression Sunrise is a good example of leaving the painting loose. He was not tempted to add more details as this would have defeated the objective of creating an atmospheric scene.

Try painting many paintings in this manner. Even if you consider them unfinished, I would rather have you learn how to see large shapes and paint them only. It is all about learning to see shapes like an artist instead of the habit of seeing details.

Once you have reached this point with some confidence, you can go back and suggest smaller details with smaller dabs and flicks of highlights. These abstract shapes will suggest waving grasses, spots of dappled sunlight, and so on. The emphasis is on **suggestions of detail!**

Use a Simple Color Palette

The confident painter also benefits from using fewer colors on his palette. Why?

- Fewer decisions to make about what color to use

- Mixing colors helps your skills develop.

- Time to mix gives you time to consider your next move.

- Rough mixes contain streaks of different colors, which add spontaneous color notes to the overall painting. Try not to overmix into a flat hue.

- Saves on costs of exotic tubes of color

I prefer using cadmium colors over permanent colors. Cadmium is stronger, more opaque, and more versatile when mixing colors.

Here are a few useful tips to avoid mixing muddy paint.[2]

It is tempting to use tube colors for every hue in the scene. There are so many colors in the paint store. Surely the paint manufacturer wants us to use more colors? There may be many colors, but we only need to use those relevant to our painting needs. For a landscape in an Impressionist style, we can look at the colors used by the Impressionists. For the most part, they used white and primary colors. We have the luxury of having a wide selection, but I still want you to stick to the basics of the primaries and white.

You can begin with ultramarine blue, cadmium yellow lemon, and cadmium red light. Add titanium white. Practice mixing the secondary color. Also, the secondary colors should be desaturated with white paint. See what happens. Try mixing the earth hues of burnt sienna and yellow ochre with the tree's primary colors.

When you are confident with these three colors, you can expand your palette to include the warm and cool versions of the primary colors. I suggest cadmium

---

2.   http://www.malcolmdeweyfineart.com/blog/painting-tips-avoid-muddy-paint

yellow lemon (cool), cadmium yellow deep (warm), cadmium red light (warm), alizarin crimson (cool), ultramarine blue (warm), and cerulean blue (cool).

Then add burnt sienna and yellow ochre as convenience colors.

This palette will cover just about any eventuality.

Surprise Yourself with Color Options

This does not mean using a complex color palette. It means switching colors or using the color wheel to create new combinations. For example, instead of using cadmium red, try using alizarin crimson as your red.

Unveil the potential for discovery by getting your hands on the color wheel and trying a split complementary color scheme. Who knows what new and exciting combinations you might stumble upon?

These variations are good exercises for introducing a new color mix to your tried-and-tested mixes. Perhaps this sparks new energy and excitement in your painting.

A different subject can also spark new uses of color. For example, an expressive sunset painting can result in unusual color combinations. Perhaps a sharp green note among the orange and violet colors adds a zing that inspires you.

Keep your painting adventure exciting and challenge yourself from time to time. This will ensure that you avoid creating a creative rut.

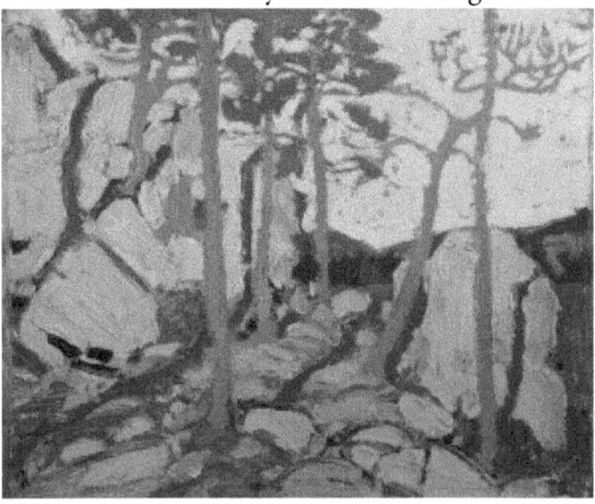

Consider this painting by Tom Thompson. It is full of bold color combinations such as purple/green and blue/orange colors working together.

Use a Painting Knife

Try adding the painting knife to your tools if you only use brushes. Not just for an occasional straight edge but also to add bold smears of color and texture. Perhaps you can do most of the painting this way.

Another advantage of the knife is that painting goes much quicker. This encourages spontaneous work. It is easier to work wet over wet without smudging lower layers.

Knife painting is an exciting way to paint. However, remember that variation of shape and texture is important. This will prevent the entire painting from looking the same. For example, distant hills and sky may need less texture than the lively foreground shapes.

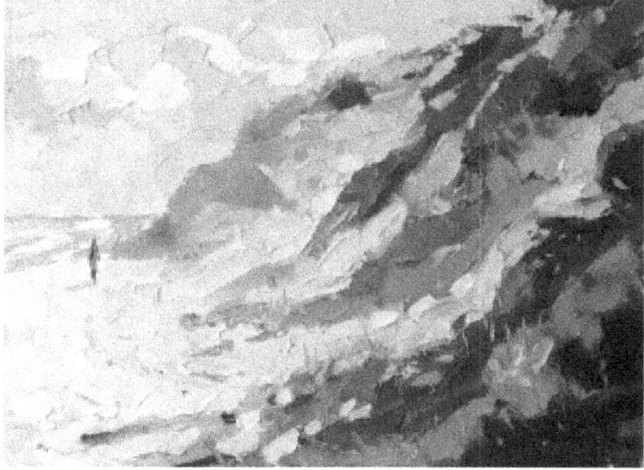

A painting knife was used in this work to add clean and vibrant color notes.

Permission to Make Mistakes

Limiting your efforts to unrealistic expectations will not give you much scope to grow. As mentioned initially, your mental approach to loose painting is critical. Give yourself permission to make silly mistakes. There is no perfect painting, so discard these notions right now.

Instead, approach painting with energy and a spirit of adventure. Be open to surprising results. You never know what you will learn next, so give yourself every chance to do so.

If your painting isn't progressing as you'd hoped, don't be afraid to revisit and revise. Sometimes, it's beneficial to let the painting rest overnight. Often, a fresh perspective in the morning brings the solution to light, and you can approach the challenge with renewed determination.

Remember that every professional painter has a history of failed paintings and will continue to make mistakes. If this is not the case, the artist is not trying hard enough.

Study the Masters

You must balance your work with studying the greats. With the internet at your disposal, there is no excuse for not researching artists. Take lessons and courses, and look for inspiration on places like Pinterest.

Perhaps you have heard of the saying, Steal like an Artist? This does not mean plagiarism or copying. It does mean assimilating methods and techniques and making them your own. Every artist has learned from those that have gone before. Even innovators like Picasso were heavily influenced by Cezanne, for example.

So allow yourself to learn new things by taking what you like from other artists and experimenting. Do so with respect and honest intentions, and you will be rewarded.

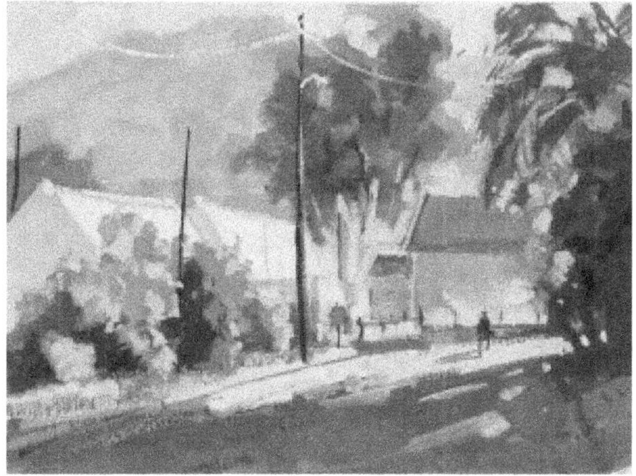

How much do I owe to the artists that have come before me? A debt of gratitude that I can repay by painting regularly. In this way I can honor them and hopefully do justice to their legacy.

More Haste Less Speed

This tip often gets artists looking at me like I am nutty. It seems like the height of recklessness to paint fast. Painting must be slow. Each brush stroke must be carefully considered and placed. Otherwise, disaster is sure to follow. Not so?

No. Painting quickly will enhance your confidence because you are not giving yourself time to think of what can go wrong. Painting loose is no place for left-brain thinking. Have faith in your instinctive talent. It is there together with your emotion and creative energy.

Preparation for painting can give you the confidence to cut loose. So do your preliminary sketch or notan study. Think about composition and colors. Then, when the main event begins, go for it hammer-and-tongs.

Don't forget to add your favorite upbeat music to the mix. Let the rhythm and flow of the music guide your brush. Combine this with using a large brush and plenty of paint, and you'll find that painting can be a truly enjoyable and liberating experience.

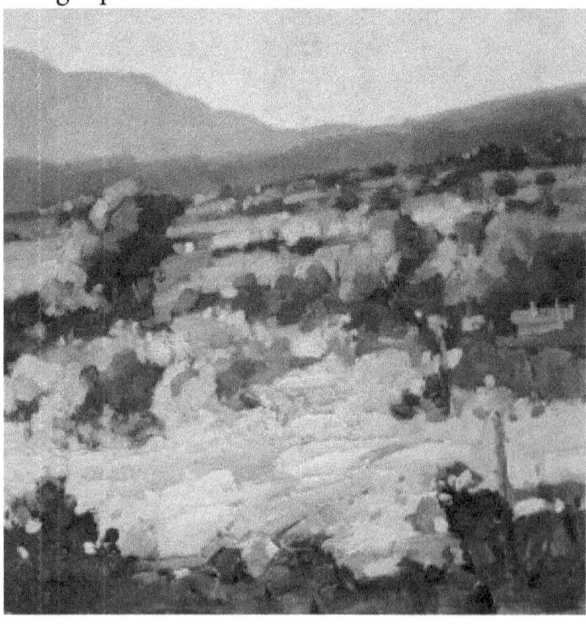

In this painting I let the brush and paint have their way. When you let yourself paint with less inhibition you can find new joy and exhilirating painting experiences.

No Painting Police

Remember, when you're painting, you're not bound by rules or expectations. You're not engaging in something dangerous or unethical. You're simply expressing yourself through art, and there's no one to blame for exploring new horizons. Believe me, if someone does criticize you, it's their misunderstanding, not yours. You may need to set them straight. This is your moment to unleash your creativity and shine.

This also goes for the split-personality types! You know that voice that admonishes you for something? Guilt perhaps? Whatever.

Get over this nonsense and live your life without fear. Seriously, many people beat themselves up like this. Why? Is there not enough drama in the world? Painting is your refuge. Your happiness in action.

Keep on painting, and you will see quick progress. If it means only on weekends, then try every weekend. Maybe you will try in the evening during the week a few times. Your painting will surely flourish. Like I said before, painting is a skill that gets better with practice.

Don't wait for the perfect time to start a new painting. The best time is right after you've completed the last one. This is the mindset to strive for. Keep exploring, keep learning, and most importantly, keep enjoying your time with the brush. The rest will naturally fall into place.

Share Your Work

Art should not be kept secret. I strongly believe that you need to show your work, whether on social media, with your family, or at the local markets. Not only is this a positive act of generosity, but it also builds your confidence. Never fear that others will not appreciate your work or laugh at you. They will not do that to you!

Also, record your work in photographs to see progress over time. This will amaze you as your art grows.

A few notes:- How can I overcome the fear of others not appreciating my work?

- **Constructive Feedback:** Seek feedback from trusted sources who can provide constructive criticism aimed at helping you grow. Learn to differentiate between helpful critiques and unconstructive negativity.

- **Growth Mindset:** Embrace a growth mindset, viewing challenges and criticisms as improvement opportunities rather than setbacks.

- What are some effective ways to showcase my art on social media? This is not the place for social media advice, but instead, I want to suggest that you take better photos of your artwork. The quality of your images and videos significantly impacts how your art is perceived:

- **Good Lighting:** Ensure your artwork is well-lit, avoiding shadows and glare. Natural light is often the best.

- **Clear Photos:** Use a good camera or smartphone to take high-resolution images that capture the details of your work.

- **Consistent Editing:** Edit your photos for consistency in brightness, contrast, and color balance.

- What are the benefits of documenting my art's progress through photographs? Among many other benefits, such as marketing, creating a photographic record of your art's progress allows you to:

- **Track Development:** Observe how your skills and techniques evolve over time. This will help you recognize growth and areas for improvement.

- **Reflect on Progress:** Gain a sense of accomplishment by looking back at earlier stages of your work and seeing how far you've come.

- **Create a Timeline:** Establish a chronological visual timeline of your artistic journey, which can be both motivating and insightful.

Demonstration: Oak Tree Lane

Painting in acrylics

Can you relate to this problem? You have a stunning scene in front of you filled with light and color. You decide that you have to paint it. But where to begin? You freeze up and are filled with indecision. Eventually, you reach for the little brush and have a go, but the result is nothing like you imagined it to be. Somehow you lost the idea that inspired you in the first place.

Solve the Problem? Yes, we can all relate to this. The problem is that landscapes are filled with details and shifting light. Photographs are also filled with details everywhere. How are you expected to select what to leave in and what to leave out? There is a simple way to tame all the chaos of details. A method that will also speed up your painting process and make you focus on what is important.

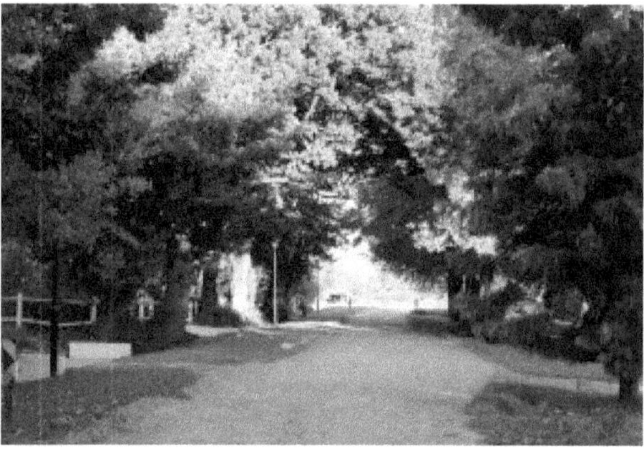

The reference. A beautiful scene filled with light and color. Also a lot of details that need to be simplified.

Think in Abstract Shapes

In this demonstration, the scene has many details. You could spend a day simply painting a tree, let alone everything else. Firstly, decide why the scene appeals to you. For me, this is about the warm light against the cool shadows and oak trees. All I have to do is make that idea show up, and the painting will be a success.

When you are faced with a busy scene like this, start by squinting a little so that you see the big mass shapes. Plan those shapes out like a jigsaw puzzle with big pieces. Really simple. Then, your job is to add more pieces with each brushstroke. You decide when the picture is complete. Let me show you how to do this.

Materials

I have a selection of Amsterdam acrylics from Royal Talens. Warm and cool colors of the primaries plus white and a couple of convenience colors like burnt sienna, orange, and yellow ochre. Brushes are synthetic long flat and filberts in size 8 and a flat in size 10. A small rigger brush features in the final minutes when I add a figure and sign my name. Almost the entire painting is painted with the long flat number 8. The panel is 21cm x 30cm.

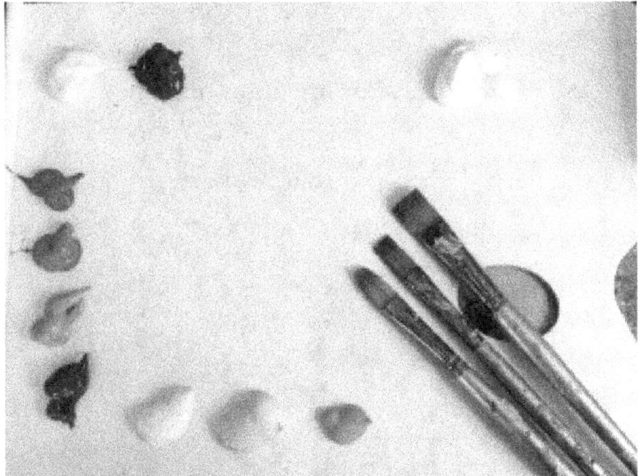

My palette of colors

How to Start with Confidence

Instead of worrying about details draw a horizon line in pencil. Then draw in the basic composition with big shapes. Then mark out the shadow pattern where the main dark shapes will go.

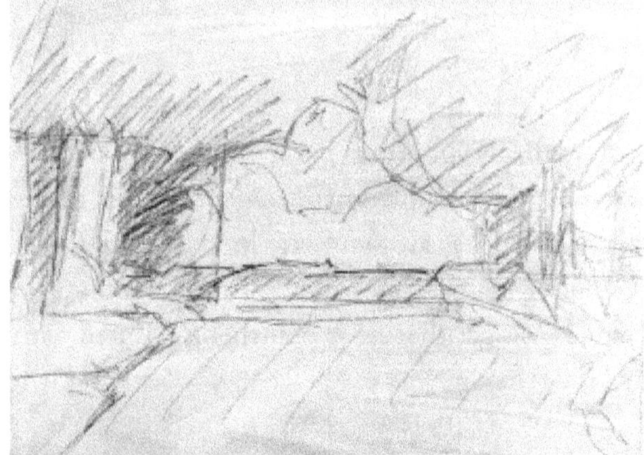

A simplified sketch helps you to start the simplification process.

Big Dark Shapes

In a painting about light, the dark shapes and shadow patterns hold the key. Establish those big flat shapes early using ultramarine and a little burnt sienna.

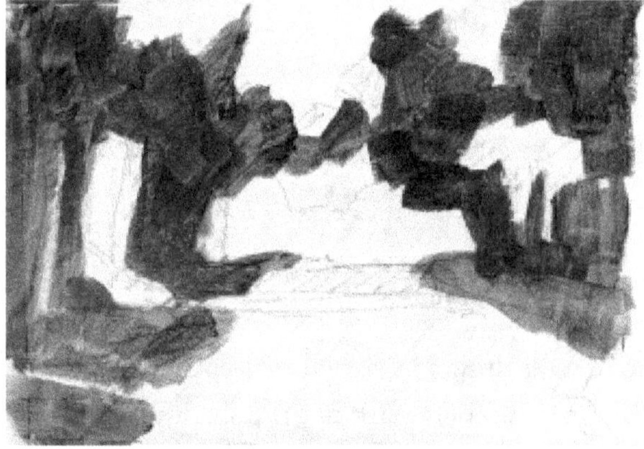

Start with the big dark shapes. Here I am using ultramarine blue and a little burnt sienna to make the dark color.

Then the Lightest Light Shapes

The next pieces of the jigsaw are the lightest shapes. I am using Azo yellow lemon with a tiny amount of white. It is important to use as little white as you can in the early stages of the painting. Especially in your dark areas. White dramatically changes the transparent dark values and cools the warm colors too much.

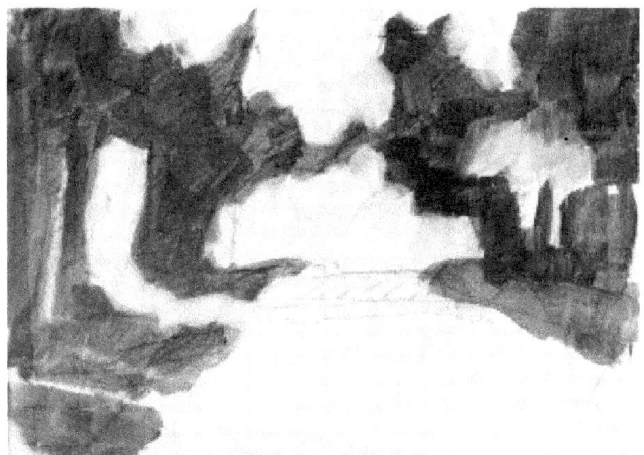

The light shapes are added.

The Middle-Value Colours

Up next are the colors in between the darks and lights. These middle-value colors cover a wide range of shapes. In this painting, the middle values are mostly the road and some of the lighter shadows, like the side of the road and parts of the tree foliage. This means you will cover some initial darks with cool middle-value colors.

I have increased the darkest shapes with ultramarine and a little orange or magenta, as the final dark pattern is now clearer to see.

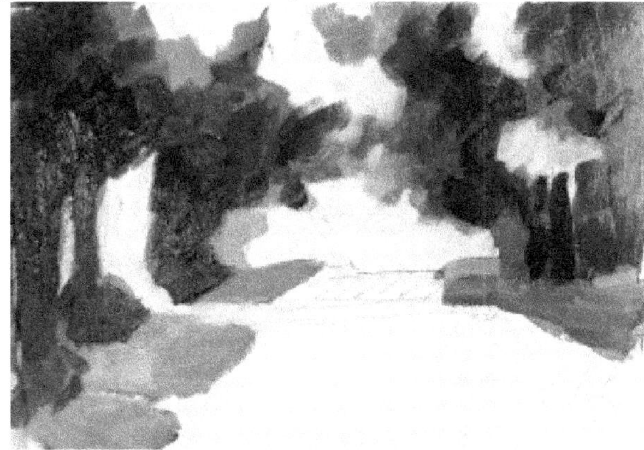

The middle value colors

Color Temperature and Local Color

Much of the road is in shadow. First, you will need to decide what the local color is—this means the foundation color itself. I have selected yellow ochre as the local color. Now, to tint it and adjust the colour temperature, I have added white and ultramarine blue. Be careful not to make it a dull grey color. Lean it to blue or ochre, depending on the temperature you want.

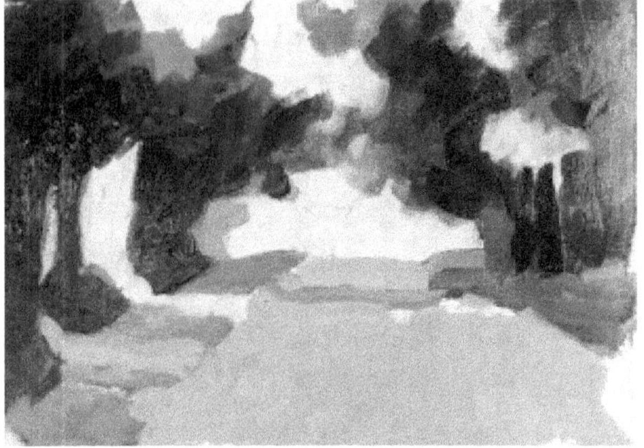

The road colors are added

Start Reducing the Big Flat Shapes

Now,, you can begin to develop the details, but still using a large brush. This adds form and volume to shapes by adding smaller shapes. For example, Orange and Ultramarine blue make a deep, warm green. This color softens the edges between the light yellow and the blue shadows in the trees.

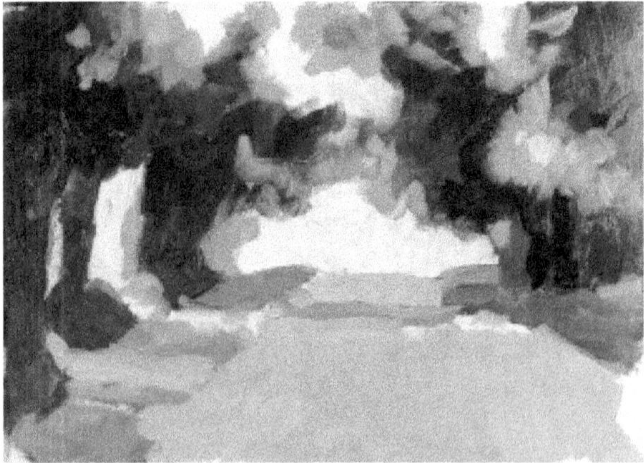

Start to develop the big shapes into smaller shapes

Add Lighter Shapes

Now opaque light yellows that are catching direct sunlight. These are warm colors but suggest green leaves in direct sunlight. Often, what we think is green is actually more yellow when in direct light.

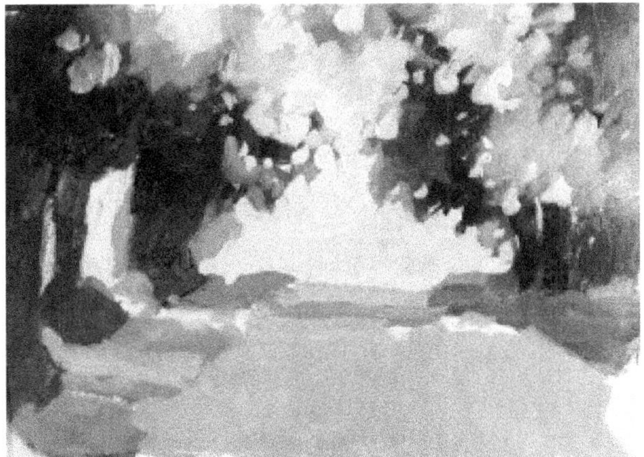

Smaller lighter shapes

Start Adding Opaque, Clean Colour Notes.

I will spend time developing the light, warm colors on the other side of the trees. The trees frame the bright light beyond. To create this illusion, the distant details are light, soft-edged, and very atmospheric. There is very little value contrast back there—almost overexposed, to use a photography term. But be careful not to overdo the white paint. Keep adding warm yellows, ochres, and so on to keep this area colorful, not cold and chalky.

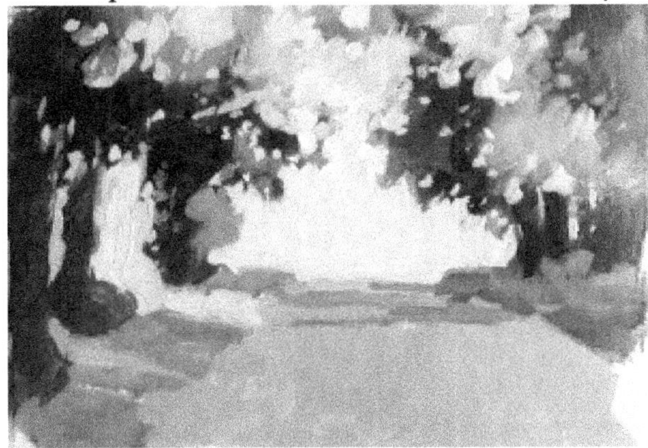

Edges and smaller suggested details get attention

Suggest Details

Avoid getting into too many details. For example, tree trunks. Too often, artists will spend ages painting in bark and twigs to get realistic trees. This simply distracts from what is important—the light. I have added a few touches of cool burnt sienna, cool reds, and oranges to add a spark or two of colour to the trees.

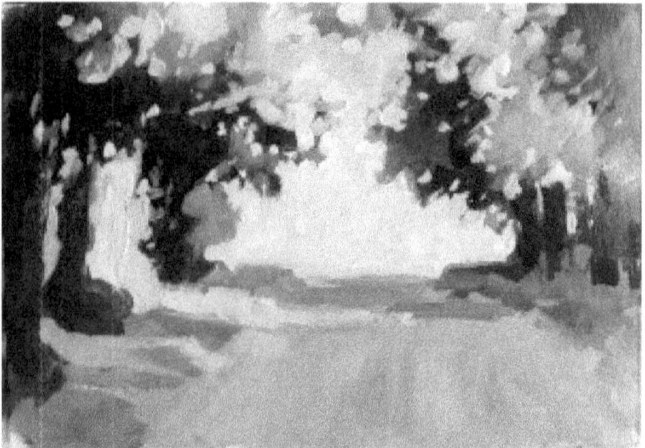

Definition and more complex color notes

Final Stages

The road gets the highlights added. I also scumble blue/violet color over the road in the foreground. This adds texture and direction lines and reduces the temperature of the color even more.

Also, add a few highlights here and there in the darker foliage to break up shapes a little more. These zings of light and color are used sparingly. Stand back, and if you get an overall impression of light and color, you know you are about done.

To finish the painting, I added a figure, a few street poles, and dark accents on the road. All the jigsaw pieces are now in place.

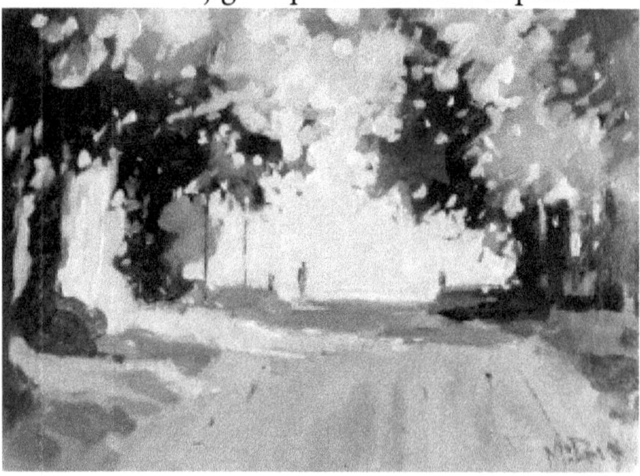

Oak Tree Lane by Malcolm Dewey

Demonstration: Dutch Landscape with Windmills

A Painting in Oils

The Dutch master artist Rembrandt van Rijn painted many beautiful paintings during the Seventeenth century. Rembrandt used his own handmade paints to create his masterpieces. He had an extensive knowledge of chemistry, which he used to create his unique recipes. Fortunately, you do not have to go to these lengths today. Royal Talens has its famous range of artist's quality paints named after the Dutch master.

With this heritage in mind, I have selected a popular scene from Holland situated in Zaandam, including windmills and water. These windmills were painted by many master artists, including Rembrandt and Monet.

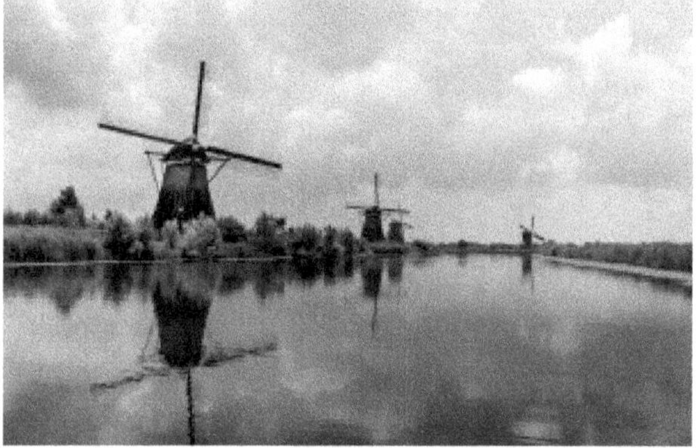

The reference photo

Painting this cool, atmospheric scene presents some unique challenges. Unlike the typical sunny South African scenes, this moody landscape is somber. The palette of colours, with its cool light and middle value colour, is a departure from my usual preference for warm light and cool shadows. It's interesting to note that in a cool, overcast scene, the shadows tend to be slightly warmer, adding a subtle complexity to the scene.

The second issue in this scene is the lack of dark-value mass shapes. The primary dark values are the windmills themselves. Most of the scene consists of cool light and middle-value color. Therefore, I must make the most of the value changes to create a strong composition.

Preparation:

To help figure out this scene, I decided to prepare a value sketch in watercolor. A sketch like this is essential to familiarize yourself with composition and important values and build confidence before the oil painting begins.

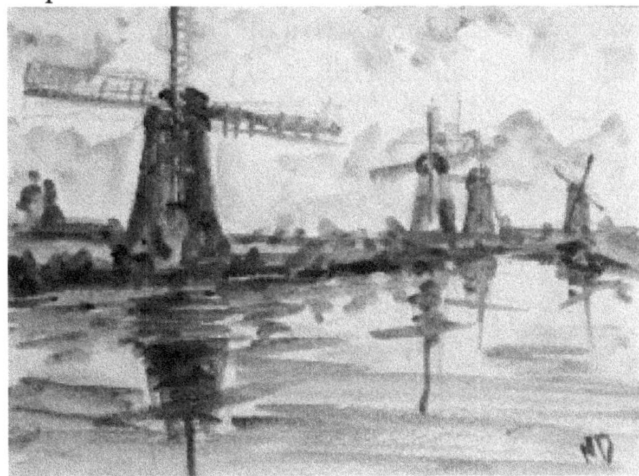

Preparation sketch in watercolor

Palette:

A typical palette of colors includes Titanium white, Ultramarine Blue, Cerulean Blue, Cadmium Yellow Lemon, Cadmium Red Light, Burnt Sienna, Permanent Madder Deep, Cadmium Yellow Deep, and Viridian. I do not use any mediums except a little white spirit to scrub in the first layer. Rembrandt paints have a perfect buttery consistency, which means you can use them directly from the tube with ease.

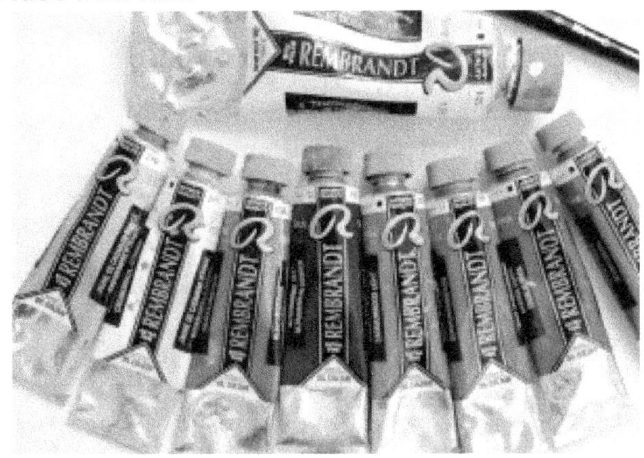

My selection of Rembrandt oil paints

Dark Value Shapes:

I like to start with the darkest darks. The windmills are scrubbed loosely with ultramarine blue and burnt sienna. The banks are dark green with ultramarine and a little lemon yellow. I am using a long, flat number 6 bristle brush. This brush keeps shapes loose and easily softens the edges of the shapes. Soft edges are important in a sweeping, atmospheric scene like this.

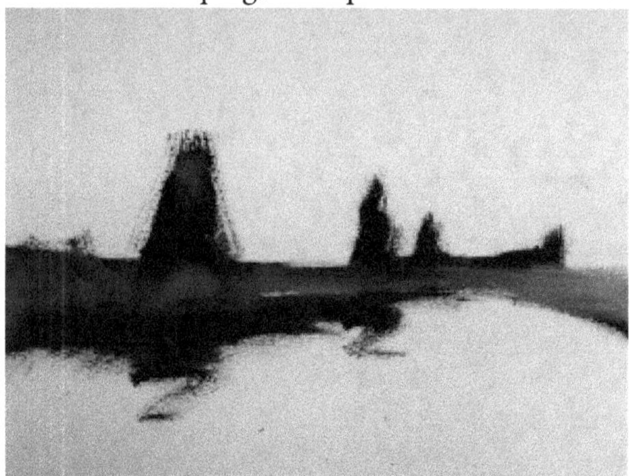

Start with the dark mass shapes

Sky ColorsI scrub in the sky colors using a mix of cerulean blue, titanium white, and a touch of yellow/green. The first layer is thin, but I intend to use impasto layers later over this thin layer. Notice also that a little madder has been added to create a pinkish color in the clouds. Ultramarine and madder are also used to make a blue/gray hue for the cloud shadows.

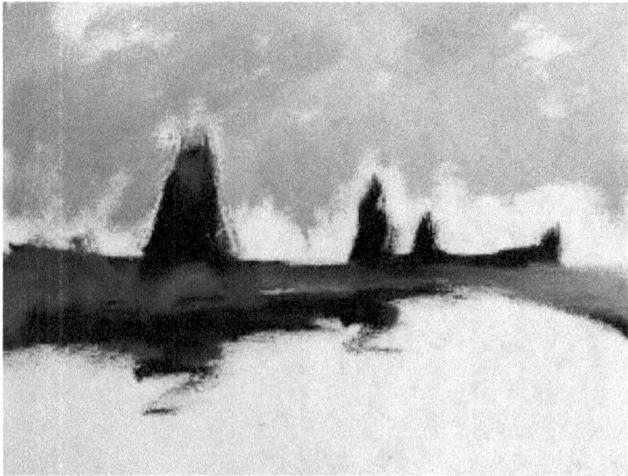

Sky colors

Sky Reflections The landscape influences the color of the sky just above the horizon. The warmer sky color needs to harmonize with the landscape, so I added a little lemon yellow to titanium white and a little blue. This creates a yellow/green tinge to the sky above the horizon. I have lightened the value somewhat to add more interest and value contrast in the sky.

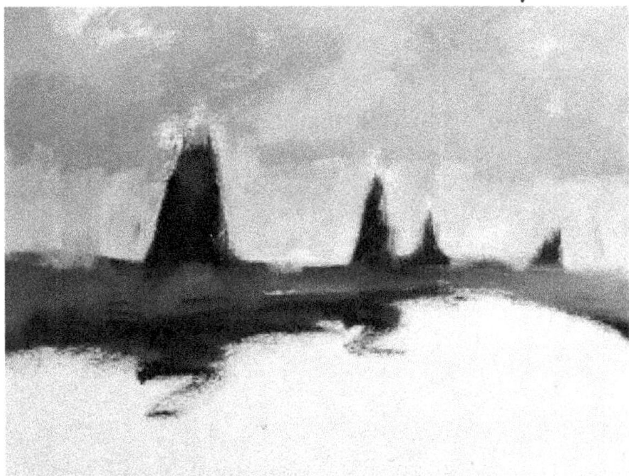

Warmer light above the horizon

Water Reflections Now drag in slightly darker and cooler reflections of sky color into the water. The windmills, as dark shapes, will reflect slightly lighter in the water. There are also greens from the bank reflecting into the water. A natural harmony of color begins to take shape.

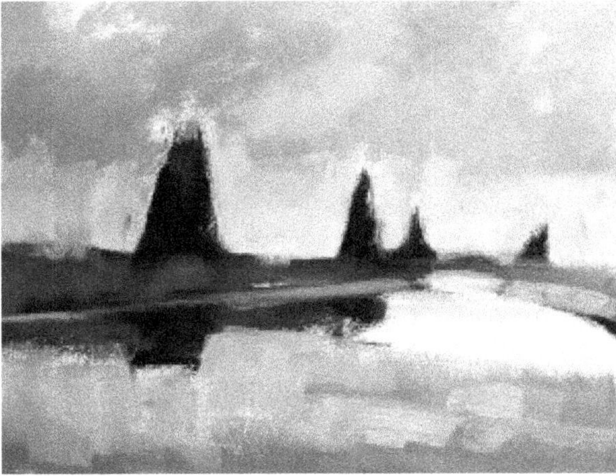

Water reflections
Landscape Elements

The landscape itself takes up a small portion of the scene. It is mostly cool, with cerulean blue, lemon yellow, and ultramarine blue dominating. More blue and white are used to create a sense of distance through aerial perspective.

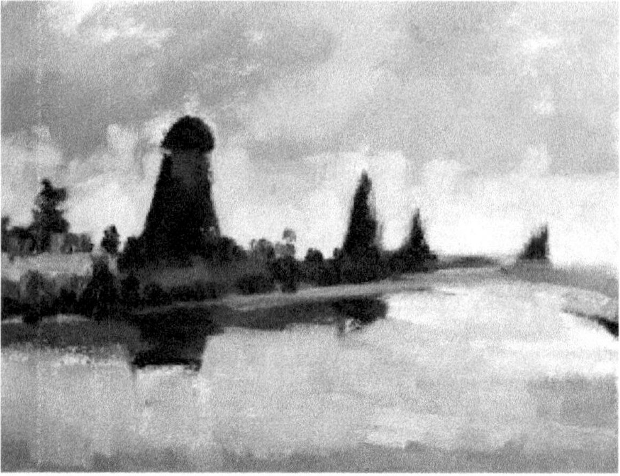

Start adding landscape shapes

Windmills and Edges It is also time to start developing the windmill shapes. The windmill in the focal area will have stronger value contrast and edges than the others, which adds a sense of distance. The windmill's colours are ultramarine and burnt sienna. A little alizarin and white add the lighter color notes. I am leaving the windmill sails for last as the sky requires more work.

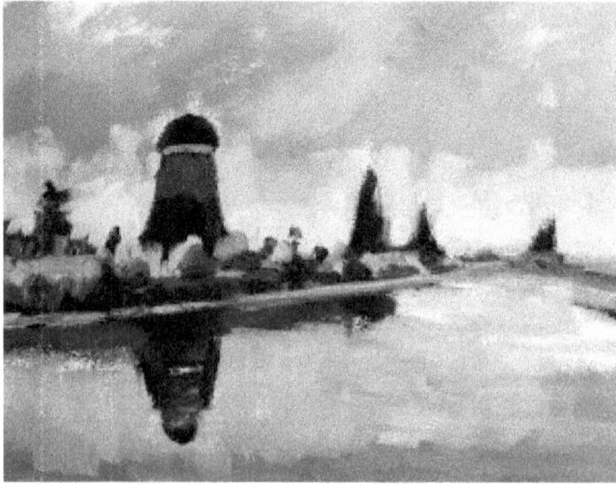

Develop the windmill shapes

Work the Entire Surface of the Painting Go back and forth from water to sky to keep the painting developing consistently. The sky gets new layers of paint. The water then has looser, thinner shapes of similar sky colour. This creates harmony while adding to the illusion of reflections.

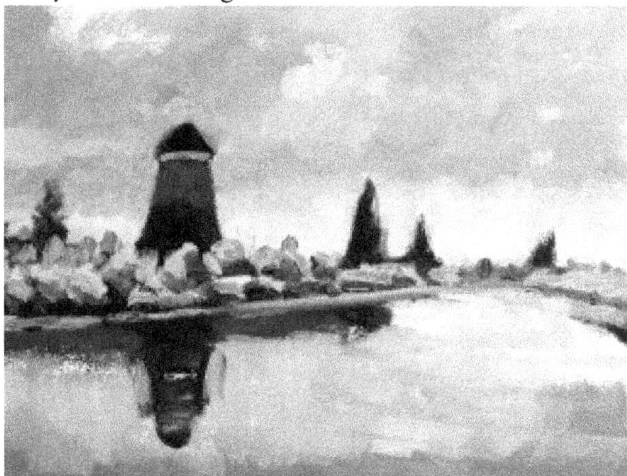

Sky Drama

Although this scene is calm, there is room for a little drama in the sky. This means working light and dark contrasts into the clouds and sky. Work out rim light with impasto layers of white and yellow. The edges of color within the clouds must remain soft. However, the edges between the darks and the rim light can be a little firmer.

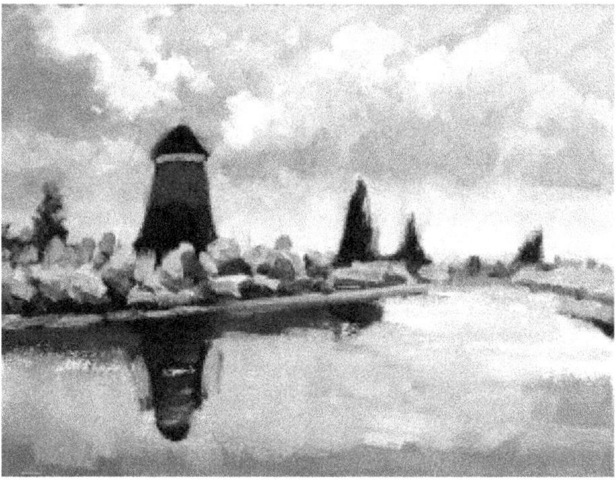

Added attention to the sky

Develop the Windmill Shapes

With the sky mostly complete, I move onto the windmills themselves. Take careful note of the shape of the windmill to obtain symmetry between the shape and the reflections. Also, note the proportions between the windmills themselves. How much bigger is one than the other? Adjust their respective sizes so that each windmill is correctly proportioned.

When these drawing issues are resolved, I can add details like the sails with a rigger brush. Make sure the sails are soft-edged. Lost-and-found edges work best to ensure an atmospheric appearance to the scene.

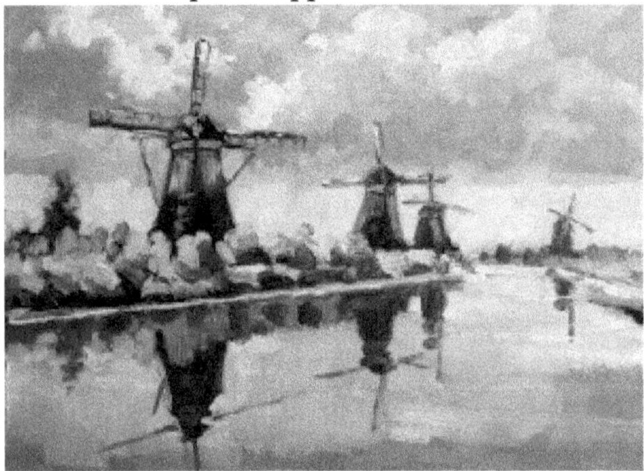

The windmills are developed further

Final Steps:

Add reflections into the water and break up the reflections using a scumbling technique. Lightly drag the loaded brush across the surface to get broken color effects and highlights. I have also darkened the foreground water to emphasize value contrast and the sense of distance between the foreground and middle ground.

Overall, the scene has a cooler atmosphere consistent with this Dutch landscape. Thanks to the bristle brush, impasto brushwork, and soft edges, it also has a painterly look.

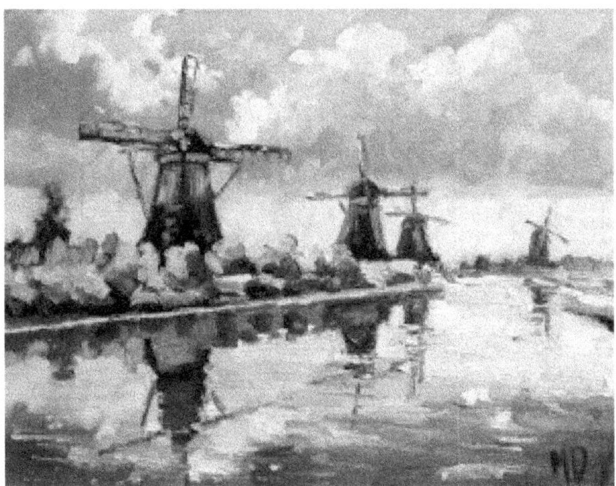

Windmills at Zaandam

Paint a Figure in a Loose Style

Outdoor Figure Study

Painting loosely may work for landscapes, but what about painting a person? What then? Do you have to tighten up your style for such a subject? Yes, the close-up figure will need a little more detail, but the emphasis will be a gesture, not fine details. You want a likeness that does not become an overworked painting, either. The gestural essence is the ultimate goal.

The intimate figure study is a fun way to incorporate elements of a portrait and occasion into one painting. I particularly enjoy outdoor figure studies because the painting has a story element. The subject could be a serious subject or something whimsical, like the subject of this demonstration today. This approach shows the subject close enough to be recognizable, but you can also get an idea of what the subject is doing.

Another plus with an outdoor subject is that you can incorporate the element of sunlight, too. In this demonstration, I want a strong light effect conveying a sense of Summer and a light-hearted mood. The reference photo captures this idea perfectly, I think.

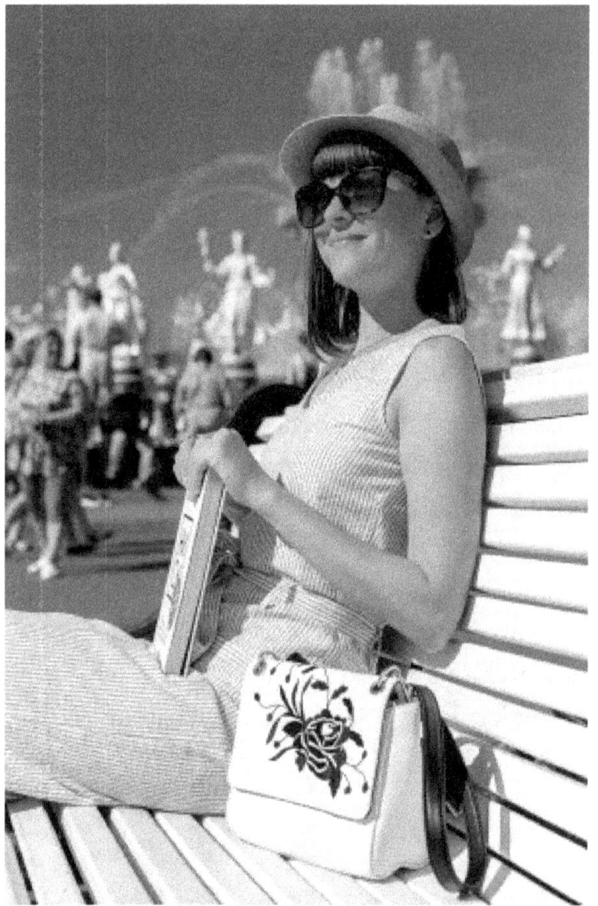

The reference. We aim for a strong light effect and capture the figure's gesture.

Drawing The most important part of drawing is looking for proportions and shape placement. Remember that we are painting shapes, not lines. There are a few approaches you can try. First, eyeball the drawing and rely on your judgment. Get one shape down first and relate all the others to it. I find this works better with a slow-drying medium like oils, where I can push the paint around a bit more.

With fast-drying mediums like acrylics, gouache, and watercolor, I may use a grid or box method to make drawing quicker and more accurate. Both these approaches are valid and work well. For this demonstration, I used a grid to place the subject in proportion quickly. When using a grid, make sure you have the same number of rows and columns on your reference and painting surface.

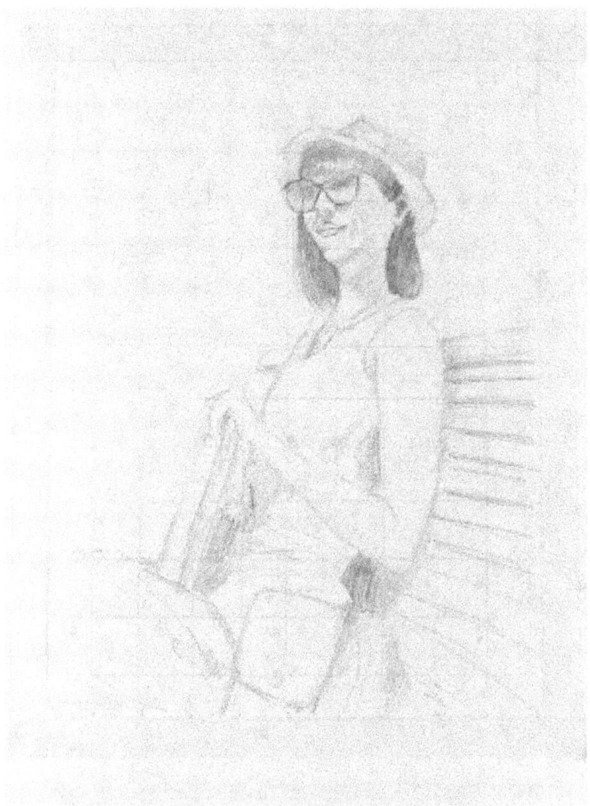

Pencil drawing with a grid to place proportions accurately

Materials Used

The Amsterdam acrylics from Royal Talens included Titanium white, Azo yellow medium, Naphthol red, Magenta, Burnt Sienna, Ultramarine blue, Orange, Sky Blue, and Yellow Ochre.

A selection of good synthetic acrylic brushes in round and long flat sizes works well. Sizes 6, 8, and 10 are best. Also, a pencil and your painting surface. In this case, I am using paper to paint on.

First Steps

Once I am happy with the drawing, I can start to block the background. A simple gradated blue adds to the sense of a perfect Summer's day. Titanium white, sky blue, and ultramarine blue, plus a hint of magenta, are used. A large brush like the number 10 flat is ideal for quickly blocking this area.

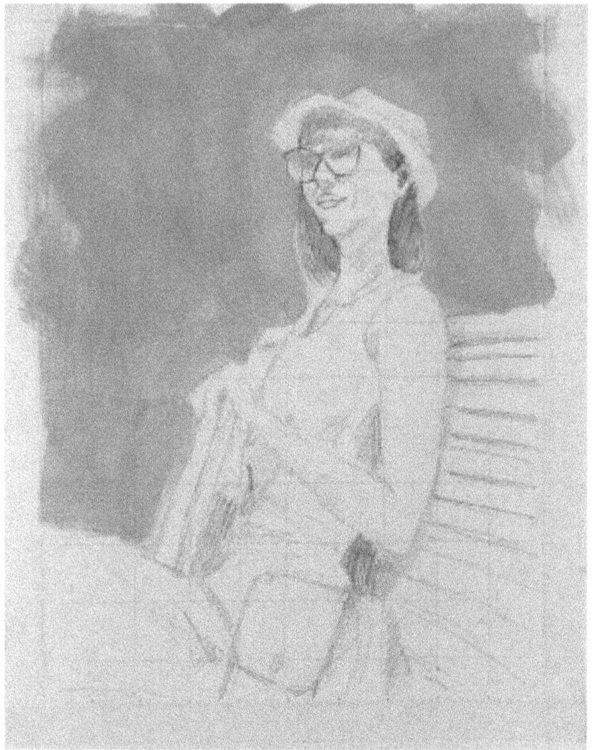

Start painting in the large mass shapes

Block in Darks and Lights

Typically, I move into the dark shapes and paint those first. In this painting, the darks are not prominent, but the dark shape of the hair is still important to frame the face.

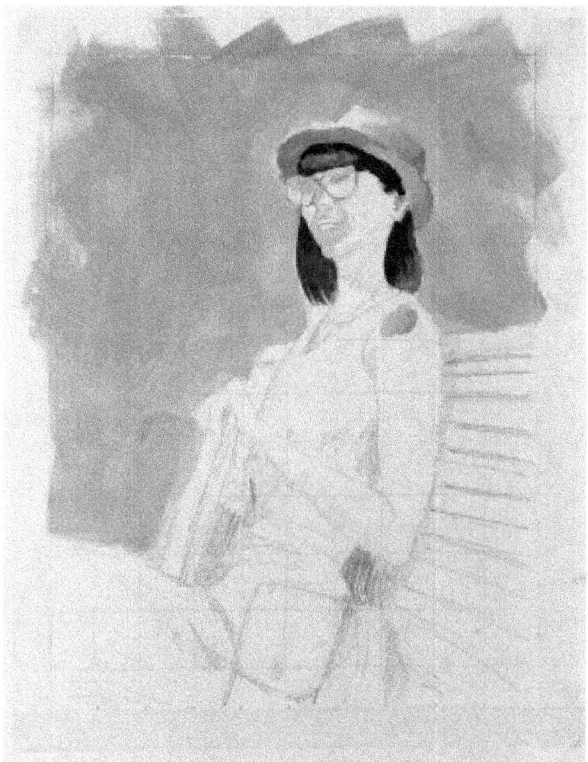

The darkest dark shape

From this point on, the painting comprises middle-value colours. I will simply paint in as many of those shapes as possible before adding the highlights.

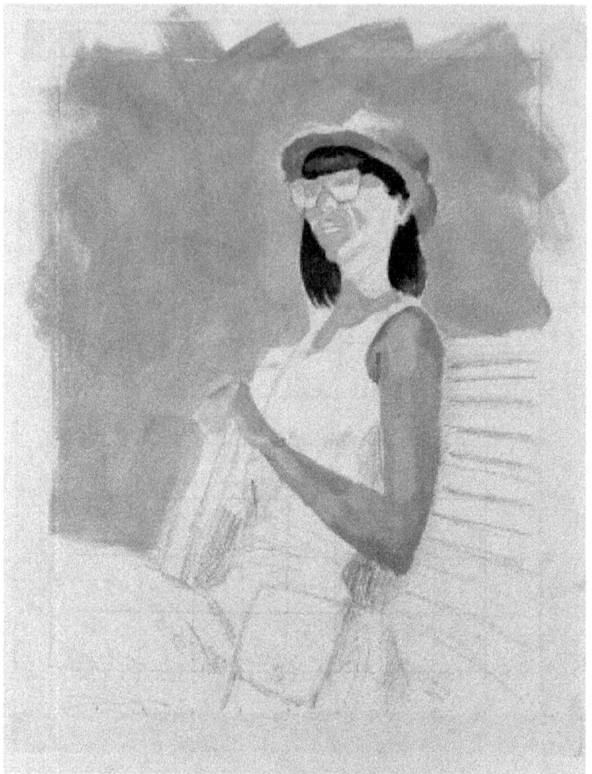

Blocking in the middle-value shapes

Note that the first layer is about shapes of warm and cool colors. Since there are few extreme values, I am looking for warm and cool color shapes. See the various shapes in the arm, for example. Instead of painting the arm one flat color, look for many variations of warm and cool color notes. Mix that color and put the shape down. You can fine-tune the edges later to make the skin tones more even.

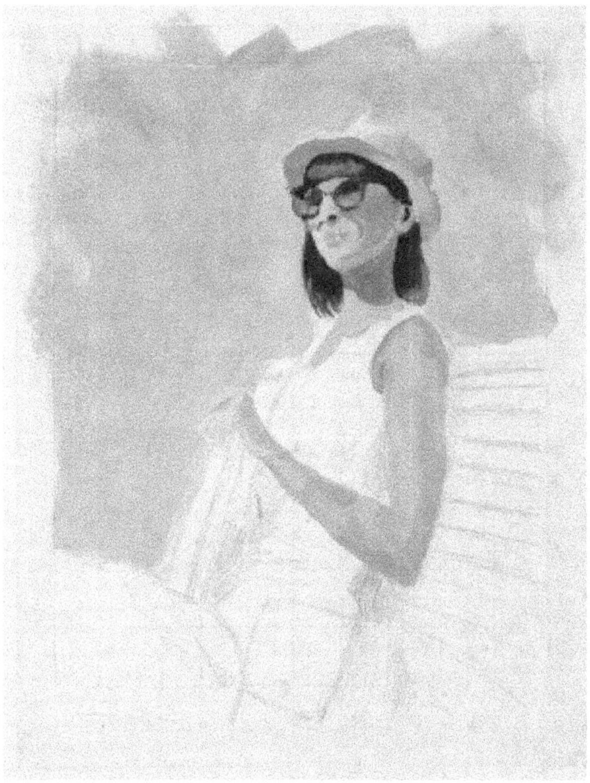

Painting the face
Painting the Face

Although this is not a portrait strictly, the subject is close enough to make a likeness desirable. However, getting stuck with the details and using a small brush is very easy. This can ruin the overall loose freshness of the subject. Not to mention leave you frustrated. My approach with the face is also to look for shapes of warm and cool colors. Paint those in quickly and adjust later. You will need to stand back to get the overall look of the painting and see what needs adjusting as you go.

Important: Do not panic if the face is not perfect at this early stage. If you feel you are getting stuck, move on to another part of the painting.

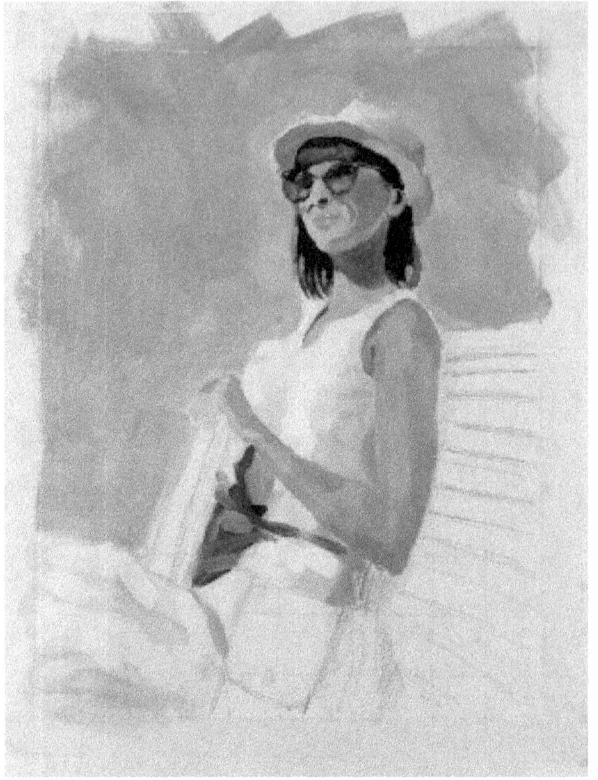

Progress to block in the rest of the figure

A steady progression with a number 8 long flat brush keeps shapes loose and forces me to look for bigger shapes. Smaller shapes come later.

I want the light on the dress to be strong and bright, almost blinding, so I am not worried about the little details on the dress, like the lines on the fabric. Remind yourself that this is a study that aims to capture a moment.

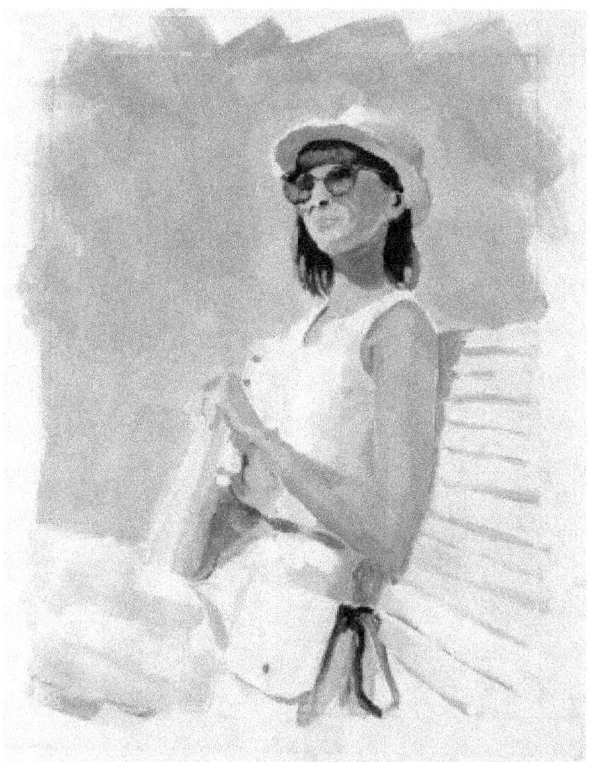

Remember strong lights against the cooler shadows

Fine-tune some of the details, like the sunglasses, and add a few highlights of titanium white and a little yellow to keep the highlights warm.

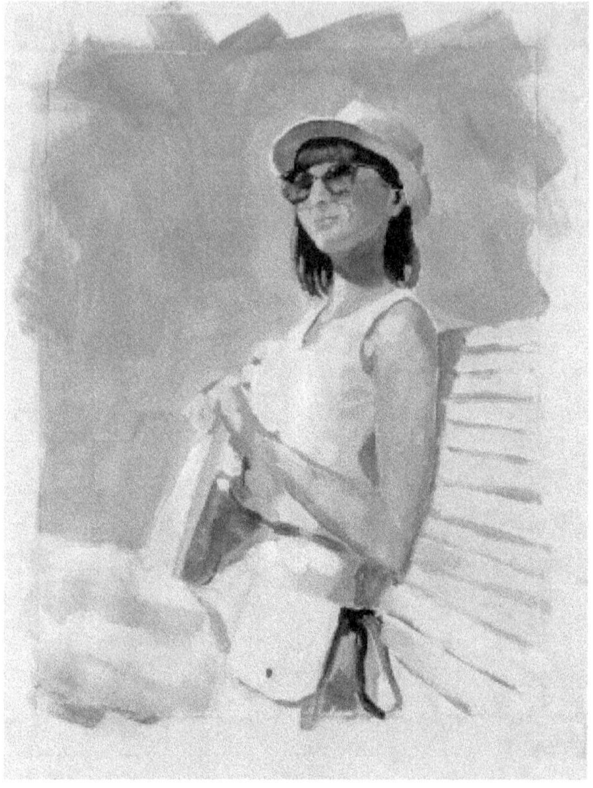

Complete details

I have added a little broken color to the background sky to complete the painting study. Also, make sure that some edges remain soft, like on the dress, book, and hands. The harder edges are around the focal area of the head and shoulders.

Final Thoughts

I want to encourage you to see all your subjects as a series of light and dark shapes made up of warm and cool colors. Also, keep in mind that light is the key ingredient. Whether outdoors or indoors, you want the viewer to see that light is present. It is through color, temperature, and values that you communicate light. This is so important in painting. The final tip is to use large brushes and a great deal of paint. Have fun.

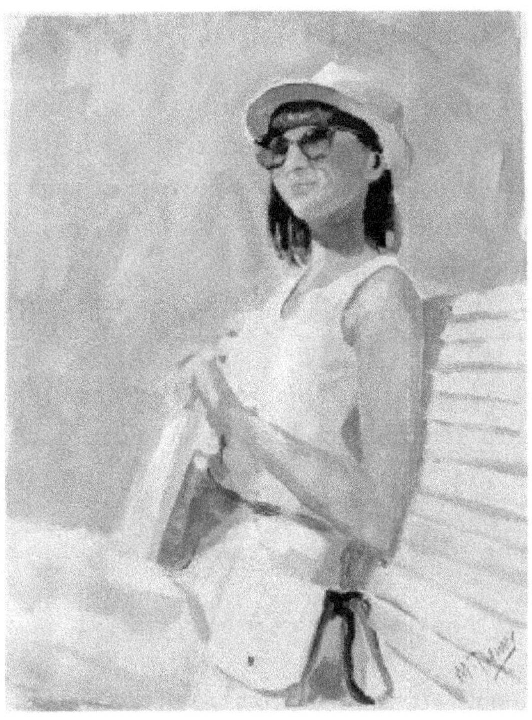

Lady in Waiting (acrylic)

Concluding Thoughts

Follow these tips, and you will see a leap forward in your painting ability. More importantly, you will enjoy the experience of creating with intention. Painting loosely is not only a physical result but a positive experience for the mind and soul. Giving yourself over to the painting gods will make you humble and more accepting of the world around you.

Now it is your turn. Are you up for the challenge of loose and painterly work? Go for it!

If you have not done so already, join me at The Artists Live Channel[1]. This is a membership site for fellow artists learning about the loose painting style.

What you can expect:

- Monthly painting demonstration covering a specific topic;

- Your painting challenge, should you choose to accept it :)

- The ability to upload a photo of your work for feedback

- Add your comments and tips

- Ongoing content about the painting process, occasional giveaways and goodies

I look forward to meeting you there! Happy painting.

---

1.   https://malcolmdeweyfineart.newzenler.com/courses/artists-live-membership

About the Author

I want to personally thank you for reading this book. If you have reached this far then you are in the "one percent" category of people that finish what they started. Maybe we can shift that statistic a bit higher? You are someone that achieves much thanks to your self-discipline. You will be enoying your life as a creatively awakened individual.

I also want to thank all those artists that study their craft with me. Whether you are a member of my Artist's Live Channel[2], own a course or watch my YouTube videos[3]. You are also self-disciplined and no doubt experiencing growth in your art. My best wishes to you!

Further learning:

My courses on painting fundamentals: Learn to Paint with Impact[4].

Now then, back into third-person:

Author: Malcolm Dewey is a South African artist and writer. He paints in a contemporary Impressionist style and mostly paints landscapes and figures. He teaches painting in various mediums including oils, acrylics, gouache, watercolor and pastels. Malcolm sells his works to collectors all over the world and his gallery can be viewed at www.malcolmdeweyfineart.com[5]

Connect with Malcolm at his website where you can join one of his free tutorials. Also Youtube/MalcolmDewey[6]

Finally if you enjoyed this book please give it a review on Amazon. Thank you!

---

2. https://malcolmdeweyfineart.newzenler.com/courses/artists-live-membership

3. https://www.youtube.com/MalcolmDewey

4. https://www.malcolmdeweyfineart.com/painting-course.html

5. https://www.malcolmdeweyfineart.com/painting-secrets.html

6. https://www.youtube.com/MalcolmDewey

Don't miss out!

Visit the website below and you can sign up to receive emails whenever Malcolm Dewey publishes a new book. There's no charge and no obligation.

https://books2read.com/r/B-A-AMPC-WESK

BOOKS 2 READ

Connecting independent readers to independent writers.

Also by Malcolm Dewey

An Artist's Guide to Plein Air Painting
How to Loosen Up Your Painting
An Artist's Survival Guide
The Creative Living Book Bundle
The Art of Content Marketing
52 Weeks of Creative Living: Inspiration for Your Creative Soul
Your Artist's Voice
52 Weeks of Creative Mastery